The Lost Boys

The Lost Boys

DANIEL GROVES

The University of Georgia Press
Athens & London

For Kit, Ralph, and Carol

© 2010 by the University of Georgia Press
Athens, Georgia 30602
www.ugapress.org
All rights reserved
Designed by Walton Harris
Set in 10.5/15 Minion Pro
Printed and bound by Thomson-Shore

The paper in this book meets the guidelines for permanence
and durability of the Committee on Production Guidelines
for Book Longevity of the Council on Library Resources.

Printed in the United States of America

14   13   12   11   10   P   5   4   3   2   1

Library of Congress Cataloging-in-Publication Data

Groves, Daniel, 1977–
The lost boys / Daniel Groves.
        p.   cm. — (The VQR poetry series)
ISBN-13: 978-0-8203-3679-4 (pbk. : alk. paper)
ISBN-10: 0-8203-3679-3 (pbk. : alk. paper)
I. Title.
PS3607.R6779L67 2010
811'.6 — dc22   2010006352

British Library Cataloging-in-Publication Data available

Contents

Acknowledgments

32 Poems: "A Trophy"

ActionYes: "Blood Drive"

Backwards City Review: "Crier"

Cincinnati Review: "The Lost Boys" (XI)

Confrontation: "Chemistry"

Country Dog Review: "Psyche"

The Dark Horse: "Penguins"

Drunken Boat: "Death of the Author"

Iron Horse Literary Review: "See Saw"

Literary Imagination: "The Lost Boys" (XIII, XVII)

Paris Review: "Portrait"

Poetry: "A Dog's Life"

Poetry Northwest: "The Lost Boys" (I, II, III, IV)

Raritan: "The Lost Boys" (VII, VIII, IX)

Sewanee Theological Review: "Work Song"

Smartish Pace: "A Stranger Here" (published as
     "A Stranger Here Myself," reprinted in *Best New
     Poets 2005*, Samovar Press/*Meridian*, 2005)

Unsplendid: "Novella"

Virginia Quarterly Review: "Way Back," "So Long"

Yale Review: "Goodbye"

To interpose the covert of your shades . . .

— William Wordsworth

I.

Portrait

I. Aperture

The monkey is the only producer of pictures who imitates
nothing . . . and recognises only the unadulterated pleasure
of the disruptive mark.
— Thierry Lenain

That old scene — monkey see and monkey do —
is done. That organizing grind, the grid,
is barred. Guerilla movements must exclude
such cagey, simian similitude,
banana republic exhibitions rid
the colony of artists. It's a zoo.

Or New World Order? Pleased to trace our line
from theirs, the prim revere a primitive —
wrenching, illuminating — by Ape X.
Abstract expression climbing toward its apex?
Creation thus evolving to outlive
our monkish copying? A monkeyshine?

We draw on our background (animals instinct
with second nature — God, the strain), that dark
age of which we — continent, prehensile
detailers, great apologists, with stencil
and rule — make light, for this *disruptive mark*,
to miss it, feeling, in the missing, linked.

II. Image

Featuring the complete line of Canon copiers
— Advertisement

Outside the window, sheets of rain, the garden;
inside, the earth-toned ceiling sprouts a patch
of sprinklers, all aligned like silver flowers
to spray the cloud-gray tiled floor with showers
(the copier, alone, may strike a match).
Temps vanish, gone to smoke. I beg their pardon.

Reflecting in a depthless black, I smack
the next original against the glass,
face down, and shut the lid — a blinding light —
its spitting image spits right up, upright.
Dual echoes, out of Catechism class,
reprove me now, my hand laid on the stack:

Salvation in the Information Age?
Or just mass reproduction? This debate
repeats itself, subsides — CLEAR PAPER JAM
(these damn contraptions). I am that I am;
a copy copies, but cannot translate
the space beyond the margins of each page.

Death of the Author

Work has to be done.
— Philip Larkin

The day's returns: our interlibrary
loaners are gathered, carted out to be
interred, in turn, as per a crisp white tag
or quaint engraving. Tip-toe quick, I hurry,
orderly fashion, past postdocs' mortuary
rigors, pronounced silences, then sag,

gasping before the corpus's deadweight —
journals, correspondence, proofs — estate
of, spineless-yet-entitled, all those (very)
loosely based on earth, bound for the next
life (for which the first is just pretext):
a morbid bid for more? A secondary

sorcery? Tomblike enscryption (tome,
"to me"), Divinely Othered ("me too," *c'est nom
de plume* diplomacy)? An undercover,
below-board plot — ex libris liberation
from restless mooning, heavenly libration
between book-ending darknesses, a hover

illuminating through all time? Depends
on meaning being read into their ends.
Such is our line of work, a critical
condition (code read). The dictator/recorder,
from day one (utter chaos) called to order,
essays the final word. That said, our call

numbers, letters reference, coming age
to age, a learned borrowing; we stage
collector's items, the catalog's invented
inventory, filially file
cartfuls, in post-Cartesian denial,
of *nihil* enisled, absence represented

within a system (Congress) — seeming-pure
egoists made selfless stewards of *Kulcher*?
Martyrs to knowledge? Patrons of patrons? — yet
a few relent — withdrawn, or lost; as wary
goes awry, an order is arbituary,
moveable as type, and nothing is set

in stone. No manufactured monograph
is monolithic. Preservation staff,
shelf-life support, can do so much about
dog-ears, foxing — cooling after the chase,
the printed page's chemicals efface,
obliterate it, gradually, inside out,

causing noncirculation, codices
and decomposing authors' co-decease;
the bookworm's bite; the end sheet eaten through;
the will in solemn form, the heritage trust:
fresh kindling — all but lit, a film of dust
stamped on, *fine*; *adieu*-date, overdue.

That's overdone. The worst case, when reviewed,
will furnish writs reissued, checkouts renewed;
spirit may matter more than letter, more
than matter. These, however beaten (raise
the volume . . . hold it) keep time still, a phrase
repeats the theme — something past things; our lore,

our stacked tall stories. Holdings fall apart
but not the whole *ding-an-sich* they, in part,
in some . . . and here again, it falls to us
to make coherent. So, Philosophy —
B1: *The Monist*; that's that, through BC:
Logic; right, what follows? Nothing. Thus,

Theology — BR: a brotherhood
wherein the *Christian*'s good news plus a good
load of BS: *Bible Studies*, meet,
while HE: *Commerce*, JC: *Politics*,
and RCS, (neither Roman Catholics'
vision nor the reinforced concrete):

Depression, Suicide, join the CC
(told you so) of Archeology,
and centuries of carbon copy now,
fossil-fueled, point down to E: *The Rise
of Secular Civilization* (social-cize
and psych-*chic* energy). LA, somehow,

comprises *Education*, attending U:
Modern War, as main corporate HQ
(our headquarters, our hindquarters) commands
attention: *Human Sexuality*
(hush-hush); on up from SH: *Fishery*
to TA: *Ergonomics*, Science stands

corrected, double-checked, as if in league
with me (TAS, again, profess *Fatigue:*
A Lecture Series), queues and queues of cues,
problems/solutions — QA: *Algebra,*
Q: *Pattern Recognition*, HAS "Ha":
Statistics, never ceasing, do amuse

on one account, whose new low condescends
to catching up on ZS: *Library Trends;*
this nominal somnolency, constant conceit,
method of overwriting, correlative
"as" of AS, whereby we must relive
Literature and History—mean feat

of Anglo-Saxon ken (*y, por ciertos,*
PCS: *Estudios Hispanicos*);
Reechoing PA: public address
in *Classical Philology*, parental
guide of PG and (*con incanto*-nental
reiterati) PH (*belletryst-esse,*

baseless acid — spleen, gall), whence *der echt* West
declines, directly, toward PM: *angst-fest*;
PR: firm, mannered English; penultimate
PS: American (postscript, indeed —
this privilege, order Congress hath decreed,
stops here, to the *n*th degree, degenerate;

coherence comes unhinged, the numbers numb,
even as letters let on, *ad museum*,
that reason sponsors all, its tired and true
calling will set right the label libel,
inferred infrastructure, diatribal
initiation, *folio a deux*) —

and N: indefinite figure, variable
whose value, one assumes, is integral
(also, one's own — anonymous assign
of *Art*, that task of naming once achieved,
impressively, by the name names, bereaved,
abbreviated, via this task of mine:

to dubiously dub, to speciously
specify). Call it a day. From me
to my relief, the late shift, NE1:
Print Collector, a common binding, small,
and discontinued periodical
supplement. The work is never done.

Work Song

The graves below the chapel clock
show birth and death, like they
were timecards, only we punch in
and punch out every day.

Every Sunday, pray the Lord
to cut the workweek short, He
says "Noah, Moses, Jesus Christ
all put in their forty."

But all our labor won't produce
a glorious ascension,
or any raises. Still, "a penny
saved is . . ." well, a pension.

"The paycheck of a saint" — it ain't
just patience that we lose
when both our peace *and* silver go
to pay communion dues.

The hymns lay off the common man,
though his appraisal's sung
when roll comes softly calling on
the pink slip of the tongue.

The timecards by the foreman's clock
are punched in, then about
an inch of empty space is free
before we get punched out.

II.

Crier

Ten o'clock and all is well-
timed, clockwork: spinning records (*Ring my Bell,
On the Beat*), DJ, countdown. Still . . .

Eleven o'clock and, all the while,
down to the minute, secondhand detail:
World News ticker, mirror ball.

Twelve o'clock and well is ill:
between rounds, shadows on the alley wall,
withdrawals from the terminal.

One o'clock: known all too well,
a vicious circle — *chronic*, pill, the stall —
"Unwind." Time servers ("Call my cell").

Two o'clock and all is well
that all else fails. Just watch (and just as well,
will is all to no avail).

Refrain. Go home. Till when will tell; and all
is, still; and I'll is we'll, is real, is null.
Toll, *homme fatale*, my coeval, a knell.
Here we, yearly, hourly, always, fall.

See Saw

Remember how we first got on,
the holding steady, eye to eye,
each weighted — pried? — on the lever
and (simple machinery) the fulcrum,
across the center of our tension?
The compliments (as one pretends —
c'est sans souci — frivolity)
eliciting, at length, a titter,
we started playing teeter totter.
Our gravity, our hem-and-haw,
yielded — purely physical law,
emotion doubly proving true
the old saw-sequent: *Do unto*
as you would have done unto you.
Coordinating, x and y,
we make the fixed point loose a sigh;
beloved, beau, above, below,
to opposite extremes we go,
won over, under (*one* — to, fro —
two) . . . Does wonder ever cease? Awe
expire? Imbalanced (as you well saw),
I see, too late, these views are slanted.
But, just between us — disenchanted,
then moved by inequality
(it *means the same*, to different ends —
though who's ass-end to whom's ascension?),

less inclined (so *mechanical*, from
evening to evening) to stay our leaver
(one second?), level-headed, I
to I, not going, coming, gone —

how, finally, feet on the ground, to stop,
get off, stand clear, and watch the other drop?

Chemistry

Before: base appetite and acid tongue,
turning, periodically, the table
(its surface shaking on the one unstable
support, hot soup to start . . . the world was young)
to test reactions (crude experiment),
still isolated in our element —
dependency.

After: mixed drinks and formulaic chatter
compounding toward attraction, that our manic-
depressed refinement might appear organic,
purely evolved — but *substance*? What's the *matter*?
This treatment . . . naturally, some don't respond,
confusing absolution with the bond
of *A* and *B*.

A Trophy

The saber-toothed cat (Smilodon californicus)
is the official State Fossil.
— California Government Code

On *E*'s live coverage of the old *Shrine*'s red carpet —
gushing, digging up dirt on the latest discovery —
the ageless Mother Rivers rushes out to see
our favorite nominee arrive (the profile: waist
and bust; fine feline *élan*; *piquant* foretaste
of a petite, vaguely Vegan vogue; no fur, no flab,
no flaws; plucked, peeled, crack-sealed, a rock-hard slab
in a long strip of this new season's newest black) . . .
"Who are you wearing?" . . . a twitch, one catwalk step back
to pause (before the nomenclature of haute couture,
the down-to-earth half-shrug, the sip of mineral water,
and dissolve to a spot for, dark and bubbling, *Diet Pepsi*),
so future epochs might observe her catalepsy;
the smile, with a trace of *ColorStay* — broad, carnivorous,
rigid as that of *Smilodon californicus*,
whose great, still frame was worn, slowly, worn away
to the fangs — a mantle-piece, in a rich stain, first on display
eons ago, minutes from here, at the La Brea tar pit.

Novella

A reedy melody — tripping, banal —
floats upon the incensed, disinfectant
miasma that receives my slow, expectant
constitutional along Canal.

It's catchy — today's Parade of Chariots'
calliopede procession passes by
(waves of Pacific Blue to pacify
the Krishna kids); Ozzie and Harriet's

self-righteous dudes ride out their surfeit, bored;
all *Grecian Formula* and *Tiger Balm*,
a Mexi-Cali thug extends a palm
tree's shadow, while the brazen *Gold's Gym* horde,

in demonstrating monstrous, taut contortions
of muscle (bound, if slightly, by a Speedo),
draws sighs along our replicated lido.
A groan to academic disproportions?

Socratic irony? The great unknown
guitarist jams, the cokeheads go coquettish
to music from another fuming fetish —
the belch of Hell's Angelic monotone

convulsing through a buffed-to-mirror chrome
and leather-perfect, idling motorcycle,
evokes a certain choked-up fin-de-siècle
refrain augmented by a reverb *Om*.

Out of the smog (this high, august occasion)
the Santa Monicas appear to bless
the progress — swollen, now; I must confess
a weakness for retro, alien contagion,

its bouquet (vintage 1968),
its public airing (teen-age Dionysian)
in which, in concert with our Dietician/
Gurus, we privately asphyxiate.

Boys will be boys . . . (this precious sense of pathos,
this blind conviction that — the damnedest thing —
the unlived life is worth examining).
Past "PSYCHIC READINGS: 50 cents (5 pesos),"

the setting sun sets up my parting speech —
Like, later, man (the Valley diction) — said
for guys like Will, or Todd (pure *Bill & Ted*).
I lie in wait for death in Venice Beach.

Psyche

. . . some untrodden region
— John Keats

Ahead, headland;
the ultimate bluff— projecting out from all I have left to stand
for me. Behind
its sheer face, broad tracts, their resources extracted, mind
turned metaphor;
the chiseled, picked-over, abandoned quarry; the *seems*; the *or*;
the loaded, vain
topos of topography — old prospects, points made plain,
what I said I meant
in legends, plotting, low comic relief. Now, glacial sediment,
the raw material
world, beyond those former footloose expeditions (the boring drill;
the dark earth-bed;
the untold treasure, briefly, brought to light; the fateful drop,
      the fled-
from peril). Here,
no further ground for assaying; no geminal facets glittering
      clear,
no features which await
my cutting devices; the platitude is wiped clean off the slate.
Yet, while I breathe,
all is self-flattery, long-winded drafts, and underneath
is overblown,
well-worn, through layers of hollowed figures, from headland
      to headstone

(no more than a toss
from the depths, the surf that breaks the surface down to a
        fine gloss,
to nothing less
than its still adamant base elements, the parts of the process
of breaking down
erosion itself: Eros and I, as always, leading on.

III.

Penguins

Our feathered friends are fowl of fairer weather,
traveling minstrels, winging back and forth;
but frozen South of nowhere (their True North)
these barking Emperors in formal dress,
a well-bred colony, patrol together
a stark topography, an emptiness.

The waddling feet, the rows of black and white
blotting a sheet of white . . . only the tip
of the iceberg. That comic belly-dip
in deathly cold impels a sheer, headlong
descent — as sovereign, as free as flight —
to depths beyond the sounding of mere song.

Blood Drive

I. The House

Blood is thicker than — well, than I thought.
Watery-eyed, thin-skinned, "the whiner" begs
(fresh from his latest round amid the dregs
of humanity), as all-is-relatives,
to be alone. That isn't how they brought
their heir up. Lest he drains himself, he gives,

and thus recirculates among his own
(faint at the sight) old rumors, screening old
humors that either boil or run cold
(such type A bluebloods). Another sterile party's
needling in vain? Blushing, one is shown
to have a heart, if not quite where the heart is.

A prick of — what? Though hardly felt, the scale
of childhood is drawn: the bronzed, colossal
sun gods, the pint-sized godson-cum-apostle;
permanent waves who sip port, drag on smokes,
mix branch waters for bankers (*Fleet*) who "sail";
and, pounding *Coronas*, recycling lifeguard jokes,

St. George's upperclassmen ("Wait . . . red tide") —
a period piece, the *Lands' End* catalog
revived. Deep breath. Step-fam aerobics jog
recollection, damp spirits congeal —
walks down the aisle, namesakes born and died —
Quick, oxygen. "Sweetheart, the bloodmobile . . ."

II. The Road

The bloodmobile: St. Pete's, right after Mass.
The word of Mother being absolute,
I drive this noncircuitous, sole route:
clogged artery, a braking surge of traffic.
The heat waves rise (*Stop. Go. No Bypass*).
The noon sun beats, cardiographic.

"Go back to Mass" — the responsorial
against the pilgrimage, through Providence,
of (dark, mirror shades) the city people hence.
On Roman Holiday, reborne, said Guido
(in lay terms) violates, Memorial
to Labor Day (that Latin blood), *our* credo —

the continent, possessed, reserved. But then,
since Verrazzano's time, entitlement
has been their legacy, who claim descent
from tourists. Full colonial boatloads
settled a shore on which Re*nai*ssance men
had visited, after the Isle of Rhodes,

the name before me, up the road, today
(poetic license — "Rhode" is singular,
of course). Though, sources leak, this may refer
to some corruption: the Dutch (or Indians'? —
or *Natives'*?) word for bluffs of ruddy clay.
Whitewash? Alas, uncertain origins . . .

III. The Mission

Can forced conversion, past miscegenation
still flow from us — one-liners memorized
in strains of dialect unrecognized
because familiar? State reps, thus agreeing
to pedigree, adopted legislation
anent that foothold (whence, on yon Aegean,

St. Paul, provisioned, sought the Holy See,
and where a feudal crown's crusaders planned
campaigns to rectify the Holy Land),
to second, in prime locution, child-support
of its parentage. A fine point. Tapestry
and rose-stained glass, the Mission waits — abort?

No way. Endless procession; surfing, static
radio deny a pleasure cruise.
Station to station — Traffic-Weather-News
to New Wave, Punk, *B101* (the all-
oldies countdown), Pop Charts, White Noise, Dramatic
Readings, Evangelists, to Classical,

Latin, Gospel, Country, Folk, to Soul
and Rock — is drowned out by the buoyant pulse
of bells: St. Pete's. As idling hands convulse
in time to the hum of engines, the bluesy lurch
and roll of ocean, taking up their toll,
an ancient organ pipes throughout the church.

IV. The Point

Pure harmony, in C, a swelling crescendo . . .
rush through the motions, bail after communion
down corridors we rode to ruin in
(at Boy Scouts, Sunday school — Platonic crushes,
ghoulish rites), to end in innuendo;
lessons (daily) bred in us, first flushes

of fleshliness commingled. *Love thy Neighbor*
(the palled, white-robed donee, nameless donnee
of Brotherhood St. Pete's is robbed to pay,
in blood) — Nurse pokes in, "Next." I bite my tongue,
fill out a pink copy of the form. To labor
the point, she volunteers I'm "healthy," "young."

The throbbing vein, the alcoholic rub;
I drop my eyes — encyclicals; brochures
(paternity, diseases seeking cures,
the marriage license, blood test FAQs);
the calendar the Mariners' Booster Club
(*Go Red and White*) puts out; cookies; grape juice.

It sinks in, finally, and leaves me numb
("big baby"); moon-eyed, in some waking dream
I sigh and watch the wine-dark life-force stream
away. "Thank you," drawls Nurse (maternal breast,
Red Cross shield). From here, our goodbyes come
to — wave on wave — a suspended, familial crest.

V. The Coast

Given — lost in heartsick swoon — to gush,
the body executes hemopoietic
(Greek roots) processes. Home, I, poetic,
pour out my — wait. The coloring returns
to my cheek: the brooding, anti-body blush;
breeding; contempt; forbearance. Lord, it burns

("the whiner" arrives, to the mannerism born;
person of choler) — Air (Recirc). I merge
into a trickle, following the purge
of foreign convertibles, and see myself
beyond the Pier (that Jet Ski set forsworn,
those dustups on the continental shelf),

and Galilee (oppressive reek of fish
that local vessels drag from George's Bank) —
fuel light; the needle pointing out the tank
has just enough to compass back around
to where, revamped, this evening's childish-
but-fluid speech will soon transfuse the sound

(mosquito buzz, rhythmic cicadian cry)
of nightfall. No man is an island, no more
than the Ocean State. A coast before
me now, exposed to sun and moon (red face
and pale), to darkness neither wholly sky
nor wholly sea; the heart proceeds to race.

Way Back

Episodic family vacations . . . only one
still went along: "The Baby," whose own caprice —
expansive, interior — their outdated wagon
became the seat of (a stationary agon;
express, per-minute revolutions vis-
a-vis — that plotted triptych — Dad, Mom, Son).

Cruise control: the vehicle's auto-emotive
design — that flipped-up way back — *made* him turn
his back on where he came from, which was where
he headed also, as the impassive stare
that met his (had time permitted one to learn)
might well have shown, but — "Jesus, Mary, and Joseph . . . "

"Damn Sunday drivers," stalling. The old man —
ingenuous, explosive — pulled away
at last, outdistancing that always-close-
behind (but farther, farther) figure. *Adios,*
El Camino. The Mini-Vanish age, one day,
will leave us in the dust. Headlights began,

in grave procession, clicking on. *Recline*
from dim reflection, child, that long-rehearsed,
spectacular total reckoning, hard and fast
asleep, who saw it coming, going past,
past all recognition. Dad braked, cursed,
and bore toward the exit, hugging the broken line.

A Dog's Life

A stay of execution: one last day,
your day, old Everydog, then, as they say,
or as we say (a new trick to avoid
finalities implicit in *destroyed*),
you have to be *put down*, or *put to sleep* —
the very dog who always fought to keep
from putting down, despite our shouts, a shoe
before its bottom sole was gnawed straight through;
and sat awake, our sleepless nights, to bark
away some menace looming in the dark.

No picking up the sense of all this talk;
you only prick your ears to hear a *walk*,
or else, the ultimate reward, a *car* —
My God, tomorrow's ride . . . Well, here we are,
right now. You stare at me and wag your tail;
I stare back, dog-like: big and dumb. Words fail.
No more commands, ignore my monologue,
go wander off. Good dog. You're a good dog;
and never quite could master, anyway,
the execution, as it were, of *Stay*.

IV.

The Lost Boys

*"I don't know any stories; none of the lost boys
know any stories."*
"How perfectly awful . . ."
— J. M. Barrie

I. Game Time

"I'm him" the little kid across the aisle
pipes up at every other second, mile
after mile, and, pointing out the pick
of pictures on a dog-eared page, as quick
as Dad can turn, is made the character,
reborn at every turn, he would prefer
to be. This used to be, or, not to be
an old man, is the only game for me,
has been since rides to school on that first bus
(detailed, like Charlie Brown's shirt, or the fuzz
of the bumblebee — that busy socialite —
in black-trimmed yellow), a melodramatic light
illumining aluminum cool green
as tomb-dim dens around a TV screen,
where I, behind a one-woman one-act
(That Girl), deep-seated, played to half-distract
myself — poised for the next round, bent to see
the drawing, claim a new identity
("I'm him": to say it was to fate it so,
for many form — *per*formative years ago);
or, peering out the window, tried to scan
the pattern unrolled telephone lines ran

beneath crows' feet — a horizontal scroll,
black against white sky — from pole to pole,
seeming to fall and rise for my fixed look,
which followed them as lines in my workbook
crackling with some secret message I
never quite made out. See, she is why
(that girl, the one? the lost?) I still replay
the game, is why I take this bus today
(would long-term perspectives, worldly whys
and wherefores, presaged acting otherwise).

II. Game-to-Genesis

From bused to bused, remote from any motive
except the unacceptably emotive,
I sit, passive-digressive, as white flags
(surrounding PR reps "*My Name is* ——" tags)
are raised, and, inevitably, deathly slow,
we move toward some convention, some craft show,
some (that time already?) exposition
of — here, my sample case — an ex-position:
(omissionary?) lying face to face
with her, within a brief befallen grace
period. To love, to be loved (*sigh*):
no game — "I'm him" changed into "I am I"
and that was that — self-taught self-knowledge we
vowed to be true to; uptight tautology
sworn on our one unspeakable new name;
de rigueur mores, keeping things the same;
O heretofore inconceivable desire!
O regnant pause, conspiring to de-sire

the child-as-father-of-the-man (dystended, due)
to make it neutral, never make it new,
and thus to reconstruct (our willful wont)
Eden from need, that we may always want
in kind — no two-timing, no jealousies
(no less — this coital moral — helices
bid cell division, gametogenesis) —
turning from just-a-game to Genesis,
dating our bios by one summer eve,
anatomy — with figments, make-believe,
redressing us (what-ifs, for-instances),
an ex-existence's insistence is
intense. And what, all told, does the past teach?
A lasting predilection for pastiche;
a fact becomes affect, then disaffection
(emotion tranquilized in recollection),
the tour de force becomes a forced detour,
a tardy farce, an echologue: once more,
rebeginning — big lump in his throat
(the Adam's apple), finally ripe to quote
by memory his bit part, ripe to choose,
apply — i*dentif*y — himself, he chews
and chews it over: the "I" he said — a whim? —
he was for good seems just another him
(the man-child at a dire pass: this side
of paradise he dies of parricide),
and she, *per se* — that prime determinant —
seems impersonal, impermanent.
Is this a joke? A test? Poetic justice?
How can it be? I don't know. It just is.
And we, as such, were just not "meant to be"
so damned sure of ourselves, essentially.

III. Face-off

Turning back to the game, from that poor-outing
(turned inside out by outpouring, or pouting),
although the make-believe that made belief
inhere in us as kids, herein gives grief;
"I'm him," informed by certain memories
of "I am I" — our former certainties
that had no need to play (which time proved wrong,
and may prove right again before too long).
Meantime, the game: relocating, regaining
losses, if possible, but entertaining
visitors, ourselves (impossible
other: at once *the* definite article
and extrovert, accommodating *or* —
which, when internalized by *me*, is *more*
like it, or not) — a worthwhile endeavor,
if one may well inquire, does it end? Ever?
Or turn, from page to page, comparative,
arcane? When will the arc of narrative
(that, hopelessly romantic, the mind wills —
the errant nights; the tilting at windmills;
the damsel in *es*trus; the Quixotic quester
de la man-child, who never asks "*Que esta?*")
break off the endless round and round about,
tell-tale it straight from *A* to *B*, then out?
To be, then out, eh? When indeed. With her
gone, "I'm him," as cultivated, wither-
soever, whenever, the game allows, can thrive.
Armed with magazines, the keen-to-arrive
deadeyes gather, hunt to meet their match
(the big game — blown-up head shots); just one catch:

the heart-throbs set therein (reverse denotations)
will tick us off to final detonations,
will blow up in our faces should we pass
the mirror's fashion-mag-defying glass.
Cover to cover, as prompt, as pro tem as
(such precariously posed dilemmas)
the newest image — good fun while it lasts,
if one recovers after total blasts.
Yet the game allows as well for all
our auto-autobiographical
elect (with gossip, comment, crossword clues,
"Classic Capraesque Comeback"; "Kidman-Cruise")
no longer limited to the fine print,
conveniently. Reflected in dark tint
(the inky-windowed *Greyhound*, second lane
over, down-ramp) floats, in sheer disdain
of its newfangled canine streak, our man:
the boy who never grew up, *Peter Pan*.

IV. Dogmatist and Pantheist

Such are the options left our travel class,
foregoing hamlets, leaving Western Mass
for Interstates: 84 to 91,
91 to 95 (begun
with Age of Reason integrity, delayed
by inclinations, mid-to-upper grade
slippery slopes, depressions; unforeseen
resurfacings, construction intervene
in media res). As traffic is no-go,
the most immediate race is: better logo —

the greyhound — dogged, sleek — who leads the pack
in hot pursuit, around that oval track
(like *Wonderland*, not far from home) of rabbit,
the wiggly, trickster playboy. Does he nab it? —
hounded by graying matters while en route:
the *éminence grise*, the flannel suit,
the thrill of the chase (Manhattan), the Sport of Queens,
plus doggerel, odd lays on what he *means*;
or Peter Pan, his greenness, flitting fairy
in takeoff, highfalutin, literary
(on whom, as per derisive, cursory
ascension through the uni-nursery —
the Cult of Mary via the Law of Murphy —
ever more virginal, ever more fey,
I was raised to — post-man-child — demand
that flights of fancy never, ever land).
A pretty picture — still, the giant letters
that dwarf it? A strange conflation of typesetters
(or archetype) — Peter, the rock of *aegis*, Pan
(the Age of Raucous founded thereupon);
the saintly usher up the Great White Way
betrayed by panic? Satyr-play display
(unsung, aero-trajected tragic heroes
reappear — dispirited Pierrots
pantomiming patricentric talk)
of some pan-sexual cock o' the walk
out o' the air? (But bound to Heaven? Earth?)
Goateed and sheep-skinned, no pastoral mirth
past oral history, nor cloud-cuckoo perch
for fugitive hours, years, at play, in church,
stuck, like — Wait. Our passage, long in doubt,
resumes. Onward, to pan — or peter — out.

V. Rabbit Proof

That better logo matter — verdict? Well,
too soon, perhaps, and much too close to tell;
seeing there remains a partnership
between the lines, a New York City trip
cannot be all they coincide in — so,
greyhounds in Peter Pan? Uh-uh. Although
the story becomes its shaggy dog , dear Nana
(slobbering, mother-tongue Victoriana)
whose clumsy but well-meaning butt-in made
that window shut that severed Peter's shade
from Peter's form, and — what? It's looking less
likely, but rabbits? *Through the Looking Glass*,
and — something else? A rabbit, rabbit . . . *Peter*.
Run out of the garden. Little cheater,
leave it to him to multiply my double-
half-in-the-making. Yet, for all the trouble
a double-you, a *with* ——— draws (*grow up*
enjoins the growing demographic group) —
Panglossian paradigms, particulate
inheritence, our inarticulate
pittance: xy (prognosticate — two peas
in the same pod, metamorphoses,
mutations, more — procrastinate) and Zzzz's;
low-born, low-bred, low-brow, Hybridean,
pestered MacGregor's unchecked, checkered clan —
the game may need expansion, so to speak;
the multitudes are so *me*, so . . . unique.

VI. Making It There

Skyline, in silhouette, cuts off my stare.
Dad nudges Junior, drops the book, "We're there"
(or soon will be there, willing dupes). This city —
New York, New York — hell, *is* duplicity:
the apple of all our idleness, the idol
of all our appetite; our deicidal
deciding facture hereof hath begat an
incandescent imagery (the Manhattan
Projection): pure anomic energy;
our field of fission; boomer-town to be
bust into — nameless, atomistic nation,
en masse, in search of our Big Appellation
(an on-spot body search — start spreading, O Muse,
O melting sex-pot, bombshell, and diffuse
your light; I want to see — apart, effete —
recast, tonight, my old flame, that lit
out for these parts; That Girl that wakes up in
a sitcom, that never sleeps, with me, again).
Mushy rumors, clouded judgment, fall-
out of all the man-to-man, or all
the fat-man-to-little boy chats — "*See ya, Dad.
Adios, el campo . . . Viva la ciudad!*" —
and *uber*-over-mentioning: "*Become,
like, what you are*" (to sum it up, and dumb
it down: original syn —) "*God! Let it drop.*" —
it dropped. She saw herself out here to stop
seeing me (as now, by intercession
of heaven on earth, with what paned expression,
faint in the twilight, I do). I — to wit,
no one, whom no one knew from Adam — split.

VII. Model/Actresses

Junior and Dad stop play, stand-to: a joint
snap-up (*destiny*, its crucial point
of purchase, a *Disney* remake); just a hunch
behind, I bite my tongue before the crunch,
our common density: pass-the-time devices,
the trip (in the midforties) come to crisis.
The brakes exhale, the engine hum goes dead,
we lift our hands and rummage overhead
for some possession — "*Peter Pan* hopes you . . ."
(*Greyhound* waits to turn, Eighth Avenue) —
lights on. Alight: corporeal convergence,
gone sprightly, fares forth, furthering discursions:
fleet-footing past where girls in every Port
Authority kiosk's top-rack consort
like suspects, all lined-up to be ID'd
by — shrink-rap — the id; we thus proceed
by impulse through this nether-land — to choose
from covers issuing from *Hudson News*?
Choose (*hypocrite-lecteured* and *mon-semblabled*)
a vehicle from interchanged, assembled
parts: Ford models — T and A, hair messed-up,
lips glossed, eyes glazed, and bold-face-types pressed-up
against the glass? The *it* girl lies beyond
the exit (grandly making hers, she yawned
"*You'll get it someday . . .*"); such enlightenment
foreshadowed still recalled entitlement.
To "get it" — given us? Adults, we see,
and — whining over whom they "get to be" —
children disown that teen-age superstition:
existence anteceding acquisition

(as ". . . *Nomine*," accordingly, "No! Mine!;"
"Love ME for ME," falling into line,
"LOVE me FOR me"), begotten back before
we got for what it was we got what-for
from forebears in quick succession; got a feel
for getting the feeling; seriously, got real;
got clues, jobs, lucky, high, our one big shot
at getting — what? discovered? — and soon forgot.

VIII. Busboys/Waiters

Through the turnstiles, we soon get rediscovered;
the backlit fronts have turned — where style hovered
in airbrushed, whitewashed smiles, strapless gowns —
to blackout; strait straphangers, hangdog frowns
take in the subway window (token reflections:
expressionistic, glaring imperfections).
Facing this artificial illumination
the untrained eye can learn its proper station:
yanked into the city's cavity
for our long-standing feud with gravity;
deadpans, adjusting glasses, checking watches
above a nonsynchronic thrust of crotches;
no privileged glimpse at rare sublimity,
in general, in anonymity,
rank and defiled, seedy (one-way suction
of basic nonartistic reproduction),
I finger-drum another sweaty bar,
reminding myself how things really are
in New York ("in your face"), a blink before
seeing That Girl, not my girl any more

than friends of hers will ever picture me
as shown in visions only I can see
(social conundrums — would my more delusive
associations were not *so* exclusive),
where my "I'm him" is not the final say —
the principal excuse, of course, to play
(or play hookey) made by raw beginners,
the doughy roll called out to be breadwinners,
warmed in the red-brick of elementary school
till burned-out, or half-baked — that is, too cool.
Noted, absently, within the glass:
the present (untutored candids), heads of the class
who hear the city (teacher of every year-
book pose) name names, and wait to answer "Here."

IX. Part Time

The normal guys it seems we've met before?
Disguised as any other's metaphor —
disciples of chosen ones, some man or "-ism"
(Pater, paterfamilias), mannerism
(dandy ennui or surplus frontier gumption)
exhibiting conspicuous consumption:
the junior partners, future brokerage firm,
and those who forge — at broker ages — firm
in prior convictions, airily protean
traits of the artist as a poor young man
before they get in (glass revolving door,
security, reception) the ground floor;
the elevated stock exchange, burlesque
of type A typists tapping, desk to desk;

the mouse race — point and click, appointment, clique
and clock (the ringing hands, the facial tick),
the ticker giving out, the latest quote
from New Age daily planners learned by rote
(*Yield to the Tao*), deadline, in-box, spreadsheet,
the big, "Executive (job's comfort) Suite" —
those who, before that gravest undertaking,
making a living, work to live a making;
fulfill the woe-is-me of self-infliction
in offices of poetry and fiction,
discerning labor at true raisons d'etre
(prophets of dorm, uprising, raising debt,
penned in a bachelor pad, walls paper thin
in case the *vox pop* happens to pop-in —
the unmanned average man its paradigm —
commanding that Big Brother spare a dime).
Oh, stereotypes . . . guest speakers boomed and roared
while the system paid for room and board,
although, for understudying a part meant
for me, a prole-reversal, said apartment —
parent-controlled and heir-conditioned unit
(my play-billed, supporting caste) — was so un-*it*.

X. Style and Usage

Ad int, a stint in The Academy
made, unstintingly, a cad of me
(the Caedmon of Cow Town, the sacred him
ruminant lows of cuddly seraphim
were heard in); some loss that, ever winsome,
the Second Coming needs a second income,

and teaches (Comp) — a gilded, lowly didact;
to think he *did*, who thought he would have died, act
on faith (lofty idealist seeking loft
ideal for thinking hard and feeling soft)
in hopes it all, if he just stuck to art,
could, in a word, repair a broken heart.
But That Girl was broken-up as well, by both
the shooting-up, publicity-stunted growth
(so pre-press-kit-schizo) — horn-rims looked down
on her, the butt of Gotham (from "Goat Town"),
fresh off the farm for New Bohemia,
social-functional bulimia-
sapped, ingesting new material
to purge herself of ("still so young, so full
of life"), devouring scenery (then binges —
out of the frying pan into syringes);
no hammy heroine, chic to the bone,
might feign that madness; back on methadone,
she even talked of going home to me.
That night, she up and bought the pharmacy.

XI. Nubility Obligates

Surfaced (O feeling, revival) out of the coma,
she suffered Mom and Pop, then POP and MOMA,
to take her in again (crawled out from under
a Rockefeller Center-based trust-funder),
and — interjections, bluntly, made in vain —
renewed the *Cosmo*-politic, Ur-bane
of all existence: shopping galleries
with frigid matrons, melting calories

to fit the Chari-Benefit A-List —
hissy-fits; a has-been fatalist
will blow off steam, as I will always see things
(petty) fogged by procreative seethings;
this siren is no folkie commune-mate
dead-set to shack up (rock on), propagate;
to strike a golden oldie, marry-in
(exorbitant *exurb — a propos* Darien —
entente), and go to waste on gaucheries
like grooming Puppy, buying groceries;
has that within which passeth chauffeuring
Sweetie to miss his sports club in the spring —
my stop. The surge to make connections cuts
my train of thought from fair Connecticut's
bridal wave of rebel-deb-celebs,
which breaks (in showers) overhead, and ebbs,
ebbs into the depths of memory,
and ceases, au fond, to resemble them, or me.

XII. The Mock Epic-scene

Ah, me. The C Train rolls out down the track;
faces, having (spectrally, in black,
specular windows) shone up for the game,
I see, from outside, in new light reclaim
their secular dimensions once they turn
their backs, back to their old selves (the spurn
of the moment — undecided, gently shoved
among the numberless mass, the great unloved,
the great unwatched); up from the underground

we rise. Out of my depth, as unprofound,
as at a loss as ever at the loss
of her, within the throng that waits to cross
and stumble through the Twenties now, I bite
my tongue. Vehement to speak — no, write
about it all, I only ("ripe to choose,"
to put it into words) put words in twos
(withdrawal pains: a diction more her speed
kept her talking smack, I OED'd —
the drug of choice) — no chance their right arrangement
might overturn our sensitive estrangement?
A linear equation, balanced rhyme
might yet resolve our points of fact, in time?
An essence still might be distillable,
delectable in dabs of syllable?
(In belletrism, bellicosity —
the griping vice of virtuosity.)
A chance the Muse, the chaste immutable,
by paraphrase might sound more suitable,
pronouncing on (eerily, reverberations
gurgle — unbecoming hesitations
and moans: the "*er*" in verb, the "*ow*" in noun)
its subjects: me (inaction), her (renown)?
Repressing a rough shorthand for sex upon
the language, entering the lexicon,
I spent late hours eyeballing my epic —
omniscient, supercilious, myopic —
the single-most, or, most single-white-guyest,
deflation of Po-Mo-Romantic *Zeitgeist*.
The *in*sights unwitting (ghost)writers encrypt:
the man you are is not the man you script.

XIII. Pedestrian X-ing

"'s me," proclaims the young man next to me
into a microphone no one can see
("it's handless"); a salty hook (Snoop Dogg, in forceful
cellular replication — more remorseful
codas of Morse code) beeps from just behind,
with black-trimmed yellow taxi cabs aligned
against the curb. From outside, looking in,
listening — BEEP — I finally begin
to recognize that first bus, separated
into these hacks for hire; the black lines freighted
with messages for only me to hear,
snipped up into these chips at every ear,
to jabber gibberish as my ears burn
for what was anyone but mine's concern
(a sole, ancient pager pulses bass —
New Order — urges on our measured pace).
Passing the meter maid along her beat,
evading eyes, I ponder, on heavy feet,
the trials over which I now preside;
in second opinions preordained, presighed,
mutter away an eloquence deferred
for one last coup de grâce, for the last word . . .
the Teens, the Village; bleak as one can get,
I spell out *Bleecker*, disregard the threat.

XIV. The Tweeters

Ahead, the façade, wherein this good night's revels
are seen to hit a stride upon two levels —
below, the pale limbs flash, freeze-framed by strobe
as stoned-age club beats thump the frontal lobe
into submission, a Euro-nuerogenous zone;
above, a kiss-kiss buzz, homogeneous drone,
dark umbrage in soft, yellow light (good grief).
Entranced, a sour apple aperitif
in hand, a quick sip stinging my eyeteeth,
I scamper, undetected, underneath
the mirror ball, by dancers dressed to chill
down to the Seventy-Nines (the *sudor*ficial
feathering, aviators, snaggle-tooth
chokers — men of leisure suits); a youth
beyond our wild conceiving, costumed thus,
digs the scene, the topos posthumous;
the dinosaur, the hustle: object lessons
in double-time, rear-moving obsolescence;
a stop-and-go-go perpetuity;
the Supafly-cum-superfluity;
in fantasizing over decadence,
our raving infancy, two decades hence.
The ADDS, Nonentities have brought
everyone back in no time, back to naught.
Retro-premises, *prestissimo* —
Hip-gnosis? Refer-madness? Acid tableaux?
The best minds of degeneration gape
at its most bestial; an eight-track tape-
remixed-with-Hip-Hop-Hop, this borough's arty
March Hares' and bunnies' big unbirthday party.

XV. The Woofers

"Hey Baby, who's your Daddy?"

                        Taking corner,
I watch (unnaturally selective mourner
of girlhood, in the name of all that's holy)
her ash into an empty fifth of Stoli
(priss-pristine ice-princess? too-Teutonic
twenty?), lapping vodka-grapefruit-tonic
from this guy's cup (the smoky-eyed enfleshment
of slowly flowing heat? of light refreshment?)
She's "taking acting classes — NYU"
(why, indeed). It's "in her blood." His too.
(So *earnest* — meant to play a joke on me,
my bloodless irony deficiency?)
A parting buss; his friend grunts "Hook-up, there,
huh, Dog?"

           "Hell yeah." Dog notices my stare —
"You know her?"
(speechless, for just a moment) "Um . . .
kind of, she . . . (the rhythm builds momentum)
and I . . . "

        "Say what?"

                  "Well, I was only men — "
(the rhythm pounds and pounds; speechless again,
overwrought by her lost, ineffable . . .
ineffable . . .)

        Dog shrugs, "She's f — able,"
then squints at me, jaw-flexing, quizzical.
"Yeah, hell . . ." (the hell with metaphysical
conceit). She wags her butt. May I infer? . . . no.
"Old-school, baby, *disco*" — I never learn, though;

Dog mounts her leg, she lights up off his Sterno —
a soft-core spree of such esprit de corps
that one can either simulate décor
or step up efforts at toughed-out panache,
requitals for (*Pang. Loss*) that same pan-ache,
winning *esprit d'escalier* before the trip
upstairs — except that winners never quip.

XVI. The Remote

An independent film mak — or *auteur*,
our bitter arbiter, the orator
of "mediacracy," of fear and loathing
for fascist accessories, in vintage clothing
divests himself of his last manifesto —
"Red Hook?" — across his angel-hair with pesto:
"Greenpoint? 'The *New* . . .' *Ut*ter decay, and why?"
(his date picks at her coat — DKNY;
an eremitic-techno-critic-cum-
an-All-American-Mama-mini-cam-
criminal-manque-coquette) "I mean . . ."
(a meta-*kinema* on ketamine)
"It's so . . . (deb to *it* to debit) . . . solip*sis*tic.
I mean . . ." He sips champagne. She checks her lipstick.
An older couple opts for Nick-at-Nite —
The Cleavers, Ward and June, in black-and-white,
cleave, cleave-to; this relapsarian
fall season starts their musing (yet again?)
whether or not it feels too soon, too late,
to flee the Empire, brave the Garden State
(An excommunicable heresy?

Our fathers' founding myth of New Jer —) "Jersey?
Come on." *That Girl* comes on; that such aberrant
notions are childish thus becomes apparent.
SLEEP MODE: "It just keeps going . . ." *Click.* "Drink *Quik.*"
Click. "Trix are for . . ." *Click.* "What's up, Doc?" *Click.*
". . . and going and going" *Click.* My eyes peruse
the bookshelf contents — "*PIX* Late News
is followed . . . Midnight Movie . . ." — gamely trying
to focus: *Nick Adams Stories, Fear of Flying,*
a postcard (Brueghel's *Icarus*, perhaps),
dog tags, a pipe, highway and subway maps,
The Great Divorce, The Catcher in the Rye,
A Wilde Omnibus, two shakers, one die,
one egg-timer. My eyes begin to close
in, read the soothing blur between the rows
of books ("After these messages we'll be . . ."),
right back — almost — to what is on TV;
Ich und Du, Cards of Identity,
Stories of Dylan Thomas, Rabbit Run;
Below, eruptions, rumblingly begun,
go quiet; snug beside a Lava Lamp,
I watch, content, as *Ernest Goes to Camp.*

XVII. Over Time

Sunlight? Among the snoring aspirants,
I gulp mouthwash to chase two aspirins,
fall in with *sacer* moms on solemn jogs
and school boys paid to walk the neighbor's dogs
(who mark, as sparrows scatter, all they pass,

the drizzly cobbles, tinselly Easter grass),
then fall back and (riddling disease,
mourning sickness) ad-lib elegies —
unbearable, or, surely, premature —
for everything that I cannot endure;
on traffic islands, kids fresh out of Juvee
sell pirate copies of next weekend's movie,
No-lexes, knock-off Third-World pottery,
low-cost LaCostes, the Tri-State Lottery;
on bought-up blocks, a poor new Joe Buck stars
at pouring joe for Starbuck's coffee bars;
by Wendy's, Holden Caulfields sneer "You phony"
at such effuse, euphonious faux-ennui
(the writer *en cachette*, *pensee*-prep) whereby
we think to bless the knowledge we will die.
Of course, there are more things (the ratio
of Heaven and Earth), no end of things to know,
this street, this city — Oh, to know New York!
(if only as Hamlet once — Alas — knew Yorick);
to "know thyself" (a *Work in Progress* sign
forces a detour — slight, if serpentine),
to know and thus to *be*, to *act*, to *live*,
lacking a viable alternative.
To swallow, at last, the fruits of long indenture:
"To die will be an awfully big adventure"
said Peter Pan, who never ages well;
the oval track becomes elliptical;
the image/"I" game seems a minor fad —
Junior looks up to realize he is Dad
(a loss for which no one can make amends,
as soon "I'm him" and, likewise, "I am" ends);

That Girl? Another story . . . first, Times Square;
The Port Authority; beneath the glare
of *Hudson News*, to *Greyhound/Peter Pan*
Departures, Ticket Window (an old man
raps on the glass; the flat-blast of a horn;
"Any second now . . ."), whence I am borne
out, again, and off, by previous
feints of the forming line, to see one bus
turn, descending into the terminal — "That's us."

V.

Continuity

"The cinema is an invention without a future."
— Louis Lumière

Cast in a glossy film the head will break
character through that local chute and *"toward
the light . . ."* — Pop's camera (*Roll 'em*), delivery room.
Such setups, native folkways warn, entomb
the soul, yet that quick pulse, the eternal RECORD,
focalizes (*Cut. Print. Wrap it. The first take.*),

as per pet projects, in development
from good stock, animated cells in frame
on frame (chalk clapboard, black shutters, bicycle rack,
front gate), the bright-lit strip that reels you back
(in rushes, the daily round) over the same
square footage every coming attraction went

over, in the blink of an eye, whose blind Persistence
of Vision " — tropes" (sheer process of elim —
il*lum*ination) beckon us toward the Lumière
family factory, the fin-de-siècle premiere
of a sole image peering down a dim
aisle, past starry-eyed faces in the distance

(their flickers of recognition, their rapt peace),
out of its depth of field, at that far light.
This is your image, moving still, to live
(between the blank sheet drawn, Executive
Producer credited) in a day-for-night,
*auteur*native ending; projected worldwide release.

So Long

I *keep my distance*, watching (the way you would)
over nodding heads, from a shaded parking spot,
your burial in a corresponding plot.
Underfoot, you may be understood,
as one assumes a silence, among the dead,
reciprocal of what remains unsaid.

United by indifference to any
common ground, to the last; conspirators,
almost — I saved my breath as you save yours
(*oneself is, all told, enough, if one too many*);
we shared — exchanged — our handshakes (medium strength),
and thereby held each other at arm's length.

The party begins (that quickly) departing. Still
apart, and still a part of them, I cross
myself as they do, passing. *Sorry for your loss.*
Keep busy, and keep in touch. We will
and will not. Apprehensions, out of tact,
then self-effacements turn to face this fact

for which you are beyond forgiving me.
If there were something to take away, a keepsake
you meant for me . . . you meant for me to take
this stance for so long: objectivity,
distance. Now, six-feet even — fathomless, skin-deep —
our distance is the only thing we keep.

A Stranger Here

> *. . . that benighted city.*
> — Frank Lloyd Wright

Escaping placement, fleetingly (. . . *Brick House*),
funk follows formstone out of vacant blocks;
as row on row of more brick houses drowse
in sprawling shade, the last carthorse click-clocks
in time to when, her ships come in, the docks
were bustling — *swart, side-burned, the common boors*
unloaded wares for Clipper commodores . . .

Loaded nowheres; the Broadway (too broad, indeed)
of memory, yoking past and present — witty
or cavalier — failing what we succeed
(hard fact, brick factory in complicity
with dream, our unincorporated city,
Retropolis). Though where but this co-here
could all our incoherencies cohere?

Such as the concrete underneath my feet,
and — high abstraction — signs above my head
(downtown and uptown — both a one-way street,
but parallel): ST. PAUL and CHARLES. Misled,
perhaps, by mere book smarts, too many dead
white males, my do-it-yourselfer projects upon
historic structures (fallen, nearly gone)

the will to restoration — which, of course,
entails conversion, also; thus the former
fills a function (cart behind the horse).
That old-line statesman, gentlemanly farmer
Lord Baltimore could not provide for more
than meets the idling idealist today
of Jacobite angel-wrestling, holding sway

through centuries of tension: Druid Hill,
Greek Town; the steadfast *Bromo-Seltzer* tower,
Domino's Sugar; Pig Town, Butchers Hill;
storefront Baptist churches, 24-hour
Rite-Aid; Beth Steel, LaCrosse; a higher power,
up with the *Sun* clock-punching; rhyme, meter;
Lyric Opera House, Mechanic Theater.

Diversions, horseplay, hackwork: arm in arm,
these couples make a scene that made out worse,
decades "The Monumental" into "Charm"
city quietly declined. Perverse
horror, or pragmatism? Poe and Peirce
died poor, dispersed, as Mencken's burboisie
(ever-mercurial) sounded-off Key,

with coltish *unitas*, unto the local
heavens (blue horseshoe collar, aureole
of looming lights) for Weaver and, lo, Cal
before they took the field at Memorial
away, and picked its carcass clean. Its soul?
Nevermore? The ravings carry on
(no bardic songster, only carrion);

to join the lost cause, beat a dead horse,
drink at the Hippo (if not Hippocrene);
my (equi)vocation, mixing metaphors
for this Metapolis, moving between
READ and CHASE (at EAGER, epicene
epicenter) and backward — significantly? —
since age eighteen, from UNIVERSITY.

My twenties amid the Thirties — classic white
marble stoops to conquer, an attic room.
But thirties amid the Twenties? Forties — wait,
I-40? The Inner Harbor's recovered womb?
Through netherhoods of dome and spire, doom
and aspiration, what prestigial
detail remains of such original

old glories, grandeurs? Charm as monument?
The antiquated anti-quaint? The odd
wrought-iron frontispiece on Space for Rent,
the odd wrought-iron star on the façade,
remember, bears a load (but household god
gargoyles' stone-faced perseverance is
only to keep up disappearances).

Form follows function — will, that is, outlive
its use. Though fretwork, grating, colored pane
and painted screen — fancy, if useless — give
perspective. Elaborate frames that show their strain
(the crack, the pipes); the imminent domain
of fixer-uppers — junk supplies our fix:
the *ton* of bric-a-brac, or the ton of bricks.

Could building blocks that, layer on layer (bored,
martyred, mortar-boarded), we precast to spell,
from TIME and LABOR, BALTIMORE, be floored,
dropping, again, to BLAME and RIOT? Well,
one noticed, visiting, in those who dwell
in this *De trop*olis "an inverse pride
in not being noticed." Suicide,

like immortality, would draw too much
attention. The *National Bohemian*
natty beau fades out, with no retouch,
winking conspiratorially, man-to-man.
Suspenders, dandy moustache, frothy can —
the trademark properties, condemned, persist
for fetishist and counterfeitishist,

stung with nostalgia by some buzzword ("Hon"),
by beehive sentimentality, sickly sweet,
glazed over, overdone, over and done,
done over. My baroque-ial school aesthete
keeps the faith, invokes the Absolete,
the cataclysm, the holy trivia quiz
"as it was in the beginning, shall be, is,

without end." Greek Revival; Drag Queen Anne;
Flamboyant Gothic; Georgian; French Chateau;
Carthorse; Iron Horse; the Iron Man;
carte blanche; wrought irony; my B&O
roundhouse (its trains of thought, however slow,
linked-up to a one-track mind to run,
always on time, birth to oblivion,

Golden, Gilded, Gelded Ages hence . . .);
into the turn, the backstretch, comes the night-
mare, my railbird's dark horse, with a sense
of show, and place, and loss, to find daylight
across the bay to which — not yet, not quite —
all are brought (the racing form, the poem,
and I, perfunctorily, follow), head for home.

Goodbye

The word enacts
what it contracts:
our nicety
joins *God* with *ye*
in the same breath,
as if (since death
or parting occasion
this blessed union) —
at a loss — to dictate
a better fate
(though *body, ego*
arrange it so),
and not confess
our separateness.
And what is lost
may yet be glossed —
e, w,
i, t, h — through
wit, he looks back,
an elegiac,
self-conscious he,
grieving history
(till bid his own
goodbye), alone.
And what is gained
may be explained —
another *o* —
but does it show

an eternal circle
or perfect nil?
End, restart
play counterpart,
just as goodbye
would rectify
what has also
gained an *o* —
the living hell
our words foretell
in greeting when
we meet again.

THE

POETRY
SERIES

The VQR Poetry Series strives to publish some of the freshest, most accomplished poetry being written today. The series gathers a group of diverse poets committed to using intensely focused language to affect the way that readers see the world. A poem, at its heart, is a statement of refusal to accept common knowledge and the status quo. By studying the world for themselves, these poets illuminate what we, as a culture, may learn from close inspection.

SERIES EDITOR

Ted Genoways

VQR POETRY BOARD

David Lee Rubin, Chair
John Casteen
Jennifer Chang
Angie Hogan
Walt Hunter
Karen Kevorkian
Julia Kudravetz
Jon Schneider